Cubic Pinwheels

by Marilyn Doheny
All Rights Reserved   Copyright © 1991 Doheny Publications
Art direction, Graphic Design and Illustrations: C. Eng Design
Photography: Mark Frey

Cubic Pinwheels is a sophisticated, contemporary quilt pattern that is *softly cubic* and wonderfully captivating. This exciting pattern is a combination of two traditional favorites: the simple 9-Patch, *altered to be diamonds rather than squares*, and Tumbling or Babies Blocks. The entire pattern is created from the continuous movement of a single diamond shape tessellating upon itself. By using the information in this book along with the unique graph paper developed for this pattern, numerous additional effects with color shading can be developed and easily converted into wonderful quilt designs using strata. Many beautiful and inspirational possibilities are available. The *Diamond 9-Patch Graph Paper* can be purchased from your local quilt store, or for your convenience, it can be ordered directly from Doheny Publications (see page 12 for ordering information).

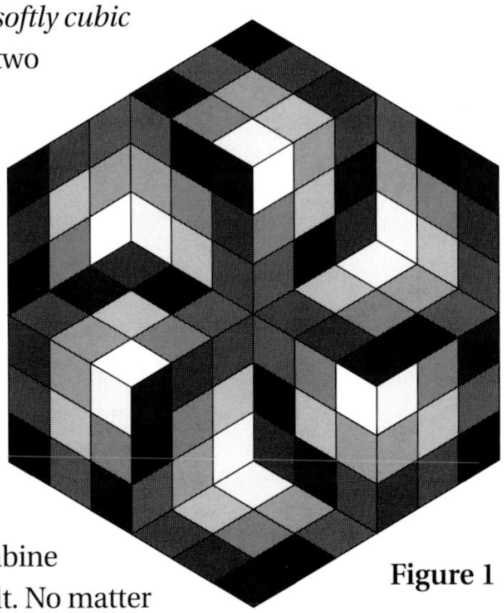

This marvelous pattern offers every quilter the opportunity to combine and incorporate numerous beautiful fabrics creating a spectacular quilt. No matter which quilt coloration you select—from a single to a six-color family composition—54 different fabrics are used, and only one strip of each! What a perfect way to involve an extensive assortment of the fabrics we cherish. Because only one strip of each fabric is used, this is the perfect quilt to incorporate the precious fabrics we have been saving because *there is very little left in our "stash."* Likewise, the expensive fabrics can be included even though we can't afford a full yard, because we can justify 1/8 of a yard quite easily!

Figure 1

YARDAGE CHART

Strip Size	Scrappy or 1-Color Family	Two Color Family	Three Color Family	Color Wheel—6 Colors*
2″ x 45″ cut size	Select 54 fabrics (⅛ yd ea) 30 Darks 18 Mediums 6 Lights	Select 54 fabrics (⅛ yd ea) 15 Dks per color family = 30 9 Med per color family = 18 3 Lt per color family = 6	Select 54 fabrics (⅛ yd ea) 10 Dks per color family 6 Med per color family 2 Lt per color family	Select 54 fabrics (⅛ yard ea) 5 Dks per color family 3 Med per color family 1 Lt per color family
1½″ x 45″ cut size	Select 54 fabrics (⅛ yd ea) 30 Darks 18 Mediums 6 Lights	Select 54 fabrics (⅛ yd ea) 15 Dks per color family = 30 9 Med per color family = 18 3 Lt per color family = 6	Select 54 fabrics (⅛ yd ea) 10 Dks per color family 6 Med per color family 2 Lt per color family	Select 54 fabrics (⅛ yard ea) 5 Dks per color family 3 Med per color family 1 Lt per color family *Blue, Purple, Red, Orange, Yellow and Green

Background yardage will be between 1/2 to 2 yards depending on the final "set" of hexagonal clusters used. No need to pre-purchase.
If 2″ cut strips are used, 5 to 7 hexagonal clusters can be created—18″ x 21″. (Figure 1 *above*, is one hexagonal cluster).
If 1½″ cut strips are used, 8 to 10 hexagonal clusters can be created—10″ x 11⅔″. (Figure 1 *above*, is one hexagonal cluster).
If more clusters are desired, create two "sets" of strata. Cut two strips of each fabric for a total of 108 strips.
It may be necessary to purchase 1/4 yard per cloth. See **Yardage Considerations** and **Yardage Adjustments**, pages 3 & 4.

Acknowledgments: I want to thank Liz Thoman for her inspirational *Amethysts and Emeralds* along with every talented quilter/friend who worked with me in the 12 Month Series and submitted their quilts for photographic consideration in this book. It was a delight as well as a difficulty to narrow the field from all of the wonderful choices. A special congratulations to the four generous quilters whose work was selected to feature the Cubic Pinwheels pattern variations—take a bow!

CUBIC PINWHEELS

Cubic Pinwheels has the effect of being "softly cubic," while moving in a pinwheel motion. To achieve both effects simultaneously, a diamond 9-patch surface with unique value shading has been superimposed within each diamond of a 60° cubic arrangement. The soft cubic illusion is achieved by using light, medium and dark values together within each diamond surface, rather than having only one value per surface as are the historic quilts we call *Tumbling Blocks* and *Babies Blocks*. The pinwheel motion comes from positioning the darker values of each 9-patch surface to concentrate along the *"long outside edge"* of the 9-patch diamond structure. By merging the two traditional patterns into one and using diffused fabric values within each diamond 9-patch, Cubic Pinwheels emerges as a visually captivating contemporary quilt for the 1990's.

IT'S EASY

From start to finish, creating the entire quilt is quick and delightful. Only straight line cutting and sewing are required. Although the entire surface is composed of diamonds, you will never have to handle or manage an individual diamond! Clever strata units are created, making it possible for all of the fabrics and the diamonds to be organized with a minimum of effort. The quilt top can be finished and enjoyed in a short amount of time. All you have to do is select 54 beautiful fabrics to begin…a quilter's delight!

Figure 2

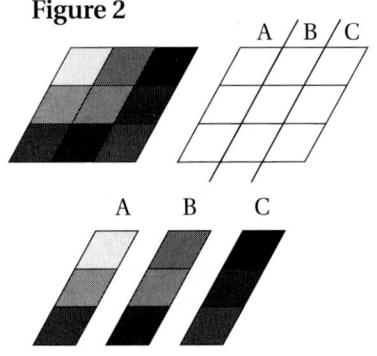

UNDERSTANDING THE PATTERN

Even though the shading for Cubic Pinwheels is illusive and sophisticated, the effect is easily achieved with the simple creation of only three different strata units. That's all—three different strata arrangements. Look at the diamond 9-patch (Figure 2). View it as three rows of diamonds rather than nine individual diamonds. When seen this way, the simplicity of the strata requirements come to life! There are three different rows. Each row is a different assortment of values. Therefore, each of the three strata units requires a different assortment and arrangement of light, medium, and dark fabrics (Figure 3). *Every 9-patch diamond in the entire quilt is consistent with the same value arrangement of this 9-patch diamond.*

In order to have a variety of these 9-patch diamonds, several strata units are created for each A, B and C strata arrangement. There are 18 strata units total—six per value arrangement—six A's, six B's and six C's. This pattern is eloquently simple at its essence! Be sure to select exciting and wonderful fabrics to keep everyone's eyes entertained when viewing the finished quilt.

Figure 3

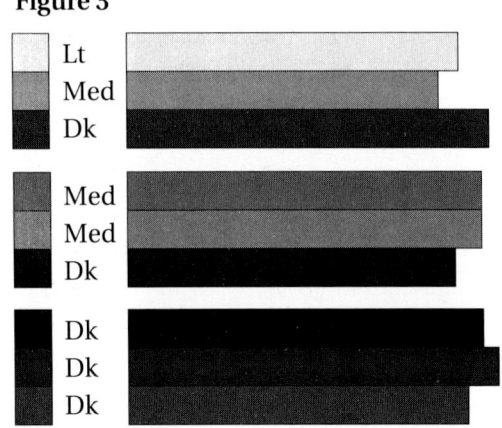

FABRIC REQUIREMENTS

The fabrics must be selected and used by value. It is essential to use three clear-cut value categories: *extremely* light, *distinctly* medium and *very* dark. To create the most alluring quilt, 54 different fabrics are used, and only one strip of each fabric is required. A total of 36 darks, 18 mediums and 6 lights are needed for the overall composition. Color designing opportunities using the 54 fabrics are abundant.

COLOR WITHIN THE PATTERN

It is possible to use fabric based upon a scrappy approach, or to focus on a single distinct color family. It is also possible to divide the fabric requirements in half, in thirds or even six times in order to create Cubic Pinwheels with different color effects. By using the unique graph paper especially designed for Cubic Pinwheels, it becomes apparent that the use of color within the pattern offers numerous delightful options!

Cubic Pinwheels provides diverse opportunities to express color within the pattern. The variety of special effects using color are apparent when viewing the four quilts on the cover of this book.

Any number of colors can be mixed and therefore used as a singular theme as in **Quilt C** (*inside back cover*); or several colors can be used and yet maintained as isolated effects creating individual pinwheels as in **Quilts A** and **B** (*front cover*). If you examine **Quilt D**, you will see that there are two isolated colors, but they have been merged within some of the pinwheel clusters for a unique divisional effect. A Color Wheel effect using six different colors can be seen on page 8. All of these color placement strategies provide the opportunity to create a geometric "pattern within a pattern."

Although there isn't a photographic example, you can imagine how easy it would be to create a dazzling and charming scrap quilt by selecting all of the fabrics without regard to any specific color assortment. Cubic Pinwheels offers many delightful and beautiful opportunities to create an assortment of colorful effects within the same geometric playground.

Figure 4
A Light   B Mediums   C Darks
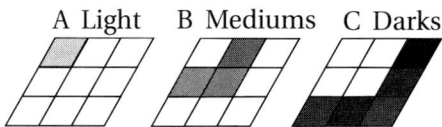

Figure 5
A. Lights   B Mediums   C Darks

Figure 6
A. Lights   B. Mediums

C. Darks   D. Full Cluster
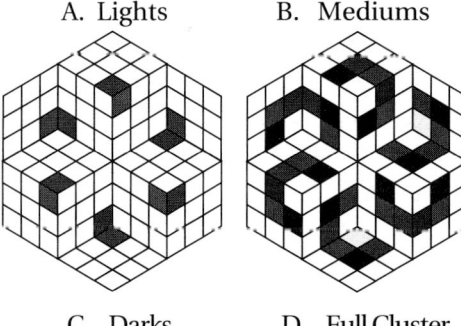

FABRIC SELECTION

Select fabrics that please you. If they catch your eye or heart, decide which value they have and include them. With 54 fabrics to incorporate, it is essential to select freely and not fret over the decision making process. It is also essential to keep the three values defined *very clearly*. Each value plays an independent and important part in the overall effect of the Cubic Pinwheels pattern.

To clarify how the values interrelate on one diamond surface see Figure 4. Then look at the corresponding cubic unit blocks showing a dark shade for each value in its isolated area (Figure 5). The effect of each value in the hexagonal cluster as also shown (Figures 6A, B & C). Once your eye has been educated to see the values as different "parts" within the pattern, view the photographed quilts featured in this book. Look at the value distinction each quilt has maintained. Each quilt artist used three distinct values while achieving a different intensity of effect. Yet all of the quilts have a different intensity due to the range and content of the assorted values.

TO USE THE YARDAGE CHART
1. Select one of the coloration styles offered: scrappy, single color, two color, three color or a Color Wheel with six color families.
2. Select the strip size desired.
3. Follow the yardage volume indicated per value.

YARDAGE CONSIDERATIONS
For both strip sizes, the yardage chart requires one strip each of 54 fabrics. This amount of fabric will create one "set" of strata.

Each "set" of strata will create:
- 5-7 hexagonal clusters using 2" strips
- 8-10 hexagonal clusters using 1½" strips

If more clusters are desired, create two "sets" of strata. Cut two strips of each fabric for a total of 54 fabrics and *108 strips*.

YARDAGE ADJUSTMENT FOR ADDITIONAL CLUSTERS

For 2" strips, purchase 1/4 yard of each fabric.

For 1½" strips, the 1/8 yard indicated *should* "just be enough". You may wish to purchase 1/4 yard to be assured of the correct amount of cloth. Use your own judgement when considering the following: a) Two strips at 1½" each amounts to 3" and,

b) 1/8 yard is 4½"

If the store cuts the 1/8 yard accurately and you cut the strips accurately, you'll just squeak by. This also assumes that the fabric does not shrink excessively.

FABRIC VALUES –DISTINCTIONS

Figure 7A
Lights

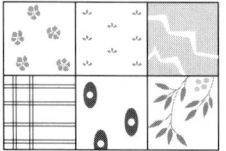

Figure 7B
Mediums

Figure 7C
Darks

1. **Be sure the lights are very light.** There are only six strips of light cloth for the whole quilt and they are essential to the definition of the pattern. If necessary, consider the lights to be "boring"—keep them simple, vague and above all, light! Icy fabric colors work well (Figure 7A).

2. **The medium category should be gentle.** Technically, anything that is not white or black is medium, so I need to get a bit more specific. Fortunately, most of us naturally select and therefore have an abundance of medium fabric. In fact, some of what we call dark is really just a strong medium. Try to stay with "middle value" mediums and be sure that *your* mediums are distinct from the darks you select (Figure 7B).

3. **Be sure to include some very dark (bloody) fabrics in the dark assortment.** This effort may seem a bit harsh for those of us who are "pastel" quilters, but several saturated darks will "nail down" the dark area by value. The dark values get watered down easily when we use the beautiful (and abundantly available) larger-scaled prints. While the larger scaled dark prints are gorgeous, they have several pockets of different colors and values within the print. Often times contrary to our expectations, they will surprise us and not "read" as dark as expected when they are cut into smaller pieces (Figure 7C).

CHECKPOINT FOR FABRIC VALUES

After selecting the 54 fabrics, stand back and view them from a distance of 6 to 10 feet. View each "value group" separately and see if the fabrics work in the value group for which they have been selected. If not, move them to another group. View the three value groups at the same time to establish that three *distinct* value groups have been defined.

ROTARY CUTTING SUPPLIES

All cutting is very simple, involving only straight lines to create the strips. The most *accurate and speedy* approach to quick straight line cutting can be done with **rotary cutting equipment.** The trio of tools is: a rotary cutter, a self-healing mat surface to cut on, and a ruler that is accurate and has visible sight lines with *double*, intersecting 60° angles.

There are many competitive brands on the market. I personally recommend investing in the highest quality products on the market for durability and accuracy to support my efforts. **Olfa Products**® are the best brand for the rotary cutter and mats. **Omnigrid**™ are the best rulers to have, in fact the only rulers with "double angled" 60° lines. If your local stores do not carry these products, we would be happy to send them to you. (See page 12 for ordering information.)

SEWING THE STRATA UNITS

Creating the 18 strata units is easy—each strata requires only two seams. Keep in mind that most distortion can be avoided if the individual strips are handled carefully while sewing and ironing. Follow the information below.

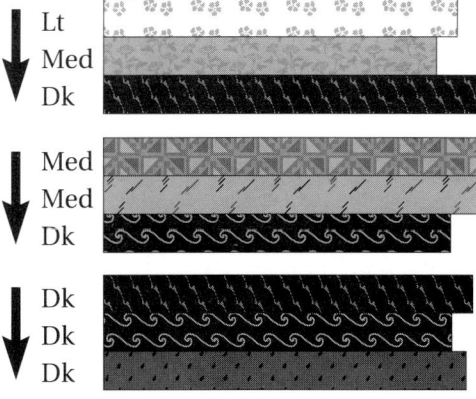

Figure 8 Prints

↓ Lt
  Med
  Dk

↓ Med
  Med
  Dk

↓ Dk
  Dk
  Dk

How to manage the individual strips for accuracy

All strata sewing for the pattern is done without staggering the strips. Simply sew them together with a 90° beginning end. The irregular lengths of 45″ cloth go to the opposite end of the strata unit (Figure 8).

When sewing strata units, it is important:

1. Not to pull on the strips. This will stretch them irregularly and cause sewn distortions called "lettuce leaves" and "rainbows."
2. To iron the seams only after all of the seams have been sewn and the strata strips are joined which makes them more secure.
3. Iron correctly and follow **Check and Correct** Guidelines.
4. Iron all seams down. Follow the arrows in the diagram.

CHECK AND CORRECT

It is possible that the strata units that you have created are not perfect. But this does not mean that they are not useful! It simply means that they need a bit of extra help. It is important to eliminate distortions as soon as they appear. The trick is in learning what the distortions are, how to correct each of them, and how to get back on track with the quilt construction.

First of all, you want to check that you have even, consistent widths of *each* fabric strip running the entire length of the strata unit. You also want to have an overall "straight" strata unit. Many things can contribute to the distortions during each of the cutting and sewing sequences.

1. If you have seam work that is causing irregular widths, now is the time to correct it before proceeding with any counter-cutting. They can be attributable to: a) poor cutting consistency, b) poor ironing, or c) improperly taken seam allowances.

a) If the distortion is due to poor ironing, then re-iron the strata to remedy "accordion pleating." Grasp the width of the strata and pull it apart to check for popping. If needed, re-iron and proceed on. The strata should be as tall, flat and wide as possible.

b) If the problem is due to poor cutting consistency, unfortunately nothing can be changed at this point. The cuts are real—they are done. Replace the strip(s) with correctly cut strips.

c) If the distortion is due to improperly taken seam allowances, then simply redo the seam from the backside. This can either be done by taking the seam allowance larger, or by removing it and taking less of an allowance. Be sure to re-iron before counter cutting.

2. You may have strata distortions that look like lettuce leaf edges or like a small rainbow arch. These can be "worked around." As you work through the counter-cutting sequences, you will continually cut away any distortion while constantly maintaining a 60° angle at the strata end.

Narrow/Wide Channel Distortion
Adjust seams to be consistent before counter-cutting.

"Rainbow" Distortion
It will be necessary to maintain the 60° angle after each diamond is cut. Trim off the strata distortion before cutting the next diamond (Figure 12, page 7).

IRONING THE STRATA UNITS

Iron aggressively across the strata seams while pulling slightly so that the fabric strips are exposed for the full sewn width. *Do not iron along the seam structures. Do not iron back and forth.* Eliminate accordion pleating before taking the **CHECKPOINT MEASUREMENT**. Be sure that all seams travel in one direction. Each seam allowance should be steamed smooth and flat.

DEFINITION: Accordion pleating is a crease that has been established during ironing by not exposing the strata to its full sewn height. Gently pull the strata unit apart to detect. Aggressive ironing (across the seams) is necessary—it causes the strata unit to attain its full sewn height.

CHECKPOINT FOR STRATA HEIGHT

It is essential that all strata units have the same overall height. It does not matter what the height is. Measure the cut, sewn and ironed height of the strata units. Measure the height of the strata unit at both ends and the middle areas; they should be identical measurements per strata. From strata to strata, the measurement should also remain consistent. Adjust as necessary to create consistency—*this is essential.*

    1. Strata units with 2" strips should be *approximately* 5" tall.
    2. Strata units with 1½" strips should be *approximately* 3½" tall.

NOTE: If your measurements are different than the sizes indicated, it is not necessary to re-do any of the seams. Continue with a consistent seam allowance for your remaining sewing efforts to accurately create the 9-patch diamonds. **This capability is a major advantage to quilt construction with strata.** *Providing patterns with built-in adaptation information is a unique and valuable feature of all patterns from Doheny Publications and Cutting Edge Quilt Designs.* We are interested in success for every quilter!

> The sewing method used thus far should be maintained for all additional sewing of the counter-cuts to create the 9-patch diamonds. Therefore, use the same sewing machine and the same seam allowance for the remainder of the sewing effort.

COUNTER-CUTTING THE STRATA UNITS

Figure 9

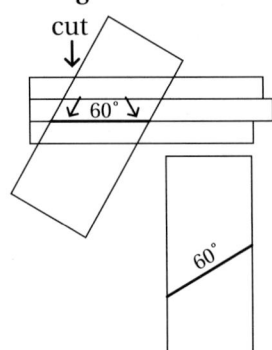

Counter-cutting the strata units is quite easy.

1. It is essential to establish a beginning 60° end angle (Figure 9).

Be sure to place the 60° line of an Omnigrid™ ruler on an internal strata seam. Do not use the outside edge of the strata unit to establish the angle.

> **Counter-cutting logic for accuracy**
> For strata, it is essential to use an internal seam as the guide for establishing any angle. Do not use the edge of a strata unit—all internal distortions are reflected at the edges of strata. It is not a "true" point from which to guide counter-cuts. A strata unit is analogous to a lake where every seam, like a water skier or swimmer, can potentially cause a rippling disturbance. These distortions accumulate at the edge of the strata as they do along the shore of a lake. The "calmest" area of both is near the center.

2. Make all counter-cuts from the strata unit at equal intervals.

NOTE: The **counter-cut width is the same measurement as your original strips.** Use the *exact* same measurement as the cut size of your original strip width.

EXAMPLES:
    If you used 2" strips, then counter-cut at 2" wide intervals (Figure 10).
    If you used 1½" wide strips, then counter-cut at 1½" wide intervals (Figure 11).

Figure 10
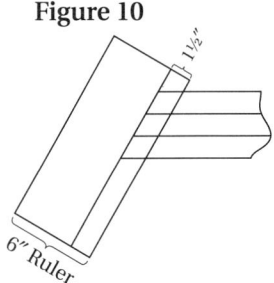
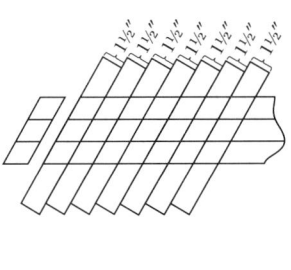

Figure 11
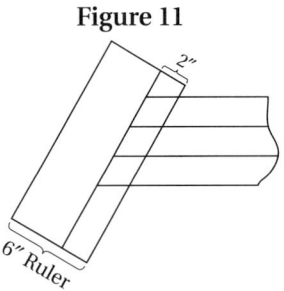
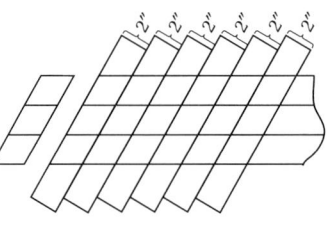

Figure 12
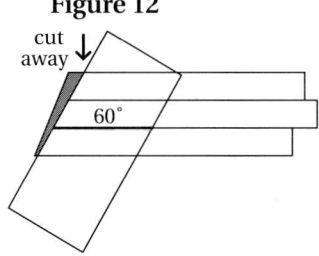

3. Check the 60° angle for accuracy after every three counter-cuts.
NOTE: Trim off and discard any fabric that does not comply with the 60° angle (Figure 12). This effort will be essential with "rainbow arch" and "lettuce leaf" strata.

CREATING THE 9-PATCH DIAMONDS

Figure 13
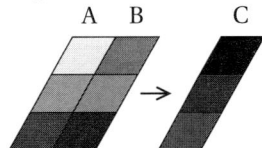
A   B   C

It is important that each diamond 9-patch does not look the same. Keep the counter-cuts from strata **A, B** and **C** in different piles. Mix and match the **A, B** and **C** counter-cuts to achieve variety within the 9-patch diamonds. Counter-cuts from strata **A** all have the same value placement. Use the **A** counter-cuts randomly and interchange them at will when sewing the three rows together. Do likewise for the **B** and **C** counter-cuts. Go for random diversity.

CAUTION: ***Do not invert*** the counter-cuts. Although the diamonds will fit together, the value placement will not be correct for the Cubic Pinwheels effect.

After the diamond 9-patch units are sewn, check for incorrect value arrangements. Unsew and correct any necessary units. Use Figure 13 to check values.

Figure 14A   14B
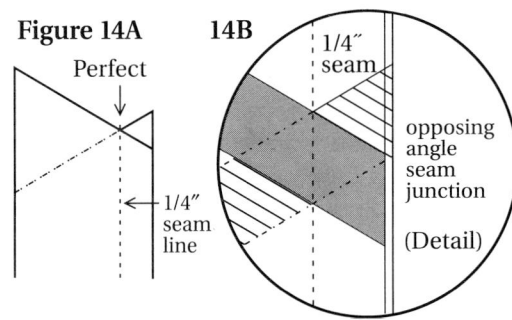
Perfect
1/4" seam line
1/4" seam
opposing angle seam junction
(Detail)

THE INDIVIDUAL 9-PATCH DIAMOND SURFACES
This sewing effort is the most challenging—there are several internal seams to match! (Figure 13) It is important to use "opposing angle" seam work when aligning the counter-cuts to start the 1/4" seam. The proper alignment is diagrammed (Figure 14A).

a) The two top edges of each counter-cut must be aligned to cross each other 1/4" inward from the seam edge. This alignment should look like the "perfect" example (Figure 15A). The seam must *start and exit exactly* this way
b) The two internal seam crossings will also occur 1/4" inward—not at the edge. (Figure 14B)

Figure 15
A. Perfect
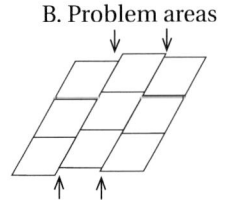
B. Problem areas

CHECKPOINT:
If the seam was taken correctly—exactly at the crossing of the two edges—then the union of the two should produce a straight line at the external edge (Figure 15A). There should not be a stair-step, upward or downward, at the edge from one to the next (Figure 15B). Check and adjust as necessary. The edges of the 9-patch diamonds must have straight lines in order to sew straight seams when joining them to create the cubic units. The internal seam junctions only need to please *your* sense of perfection!

Figure 16

JOINING THE 9-PATCH DIAMONDS
1. For every hexagonal cluster, select 12 of the 9-patch diamonds.
2. Reserve three 9-patch diamonds and use nine to create three cubic boxes (Figure 16). Be sure to keep the dark valued edges positioned as indicated.

3. *Follow **Inset Seam** information below for all circled areas* (Figures 19 to 23).
4. Continue to join the three cubic boxes and the reserved units as shown (Figure 24).
NOTE: If Color Wheel or Split Color Clusters (**Quilt D**) are required, follow the specific diagrams in **SPECIAL EFFECTS** (page 9).

INSET SEAMS

Figure 17

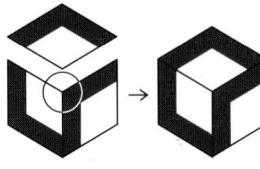

Figure 18

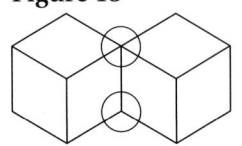

Figure 19

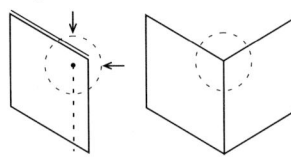

Figure 20

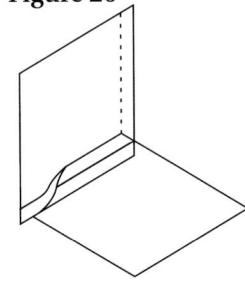

Figure 21
needle

seam A

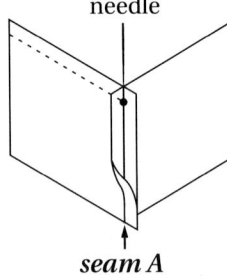

Figure 22
needle

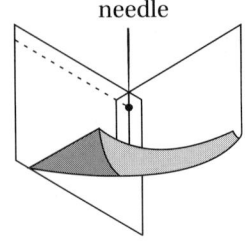

PREPARING THE FIRST SEAM

Sewing three different diamond surfaces together requires inset piecing. The circled areas represent the "inset" area of one cubic block (Figure 17). Joining several boxes also requires subsequent inset seam work (Figure 18).

When sewing seams which require subsequent inset seamwork:
1. Leave the last 1/4" of the seam (at the inset area) unsewn (Figure 19).
2. Back stitch for strength.
3. Iron the entire seam in one direction.
4. Then re-iron the last 2" of seam allowance (at the inset area) open.
5. Turn the unit over and begin to "inset" the next part by sewing from the backside so that all intricate seam areas are exposed where the inset is taking place.

NOTE: Be sure to match strata seams along the edges of each diamond unit as necessary when sewing the diamonds together. They should nestle easily. Change the direction of the seam allowances with your finger tips as necessary to redistribute the thickness and to help the seam junctions match more easily.

THE INSET SEAM

Always position the two units together exposing the underside of the project so that you can *see* the seam allowance of the inset area.

1. Line up both fabric shapes so that they match exactly to start the seam (Figure 20).
2. Leave any necessary unsewn 1/4" beginning seam areas for future inset sewing.
3. Begin the stitch from the outside edge and stitch toward the inset or pivot area (dead center of the opened seam allowance). The seam allowances should all be in full view (Figure 21).
4. *Have the needle in the fabric*, dead center of the seam which is ironed open.
5. The needle should be in the cloth just between each seam allowance. If the previous seam (see arrow) is correct, the needle has stopped exactly at the point where *seam A* stopped and is backstitched.

THE PIVOT SEAM ACTION

1. At the inset or pivot area, you will lift the pressure foot and rotate the entire unit cloth together in a counter-clockwise (not clockwise) motion. ***Rotate all fabrics together.***
2. Turn them counter clockwise until the piece being "set in" is travelling directly from the needle towards your chest. This is the "under" piece of cloth (Figure 22).

NOTE: It may be necessary to roll up the "above" fabric unit to expose the "under" fabric. This will line up the edge of the lower unit of cloth from the needle towards your chest.

3. Using your right hand, hold the "under" piece of cloth in this position on the throat plate of the sewing machine.
4. With your left hand, begin to rotate the top unit to the left and back of the needle area. To do this:
   a) maintain a "pull forward" and
   b) rotate clockwise action, "to the left and back." You may need to repeat this

Figure 23

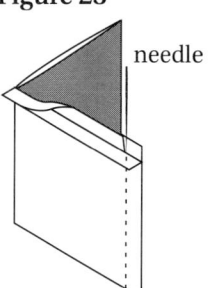

process several times if the "above" unit is large or long (Figure 23).

5. Stop the rotation action when the exit edge of the above unit and the edge of the (under) "set-in" piece line up parallel. Whichever way they line up, heading from the needle to your chest, keep both edges parallel for the entire exit seam.
6. Drop the pressure foot then: a) sew out to the exit edge (Figure 23), or
   b) sew to the next pivot (inset) area.
7. Repeat the Inset/Pivot Procedure.
8. Adding background fabric shapes to the rows of inset boxes requires continuous insetting activity as well.

Figure 24

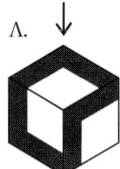
A.

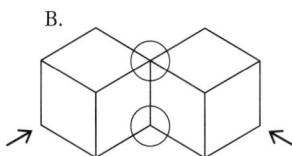
B.

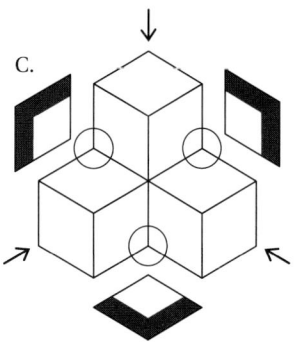
C.

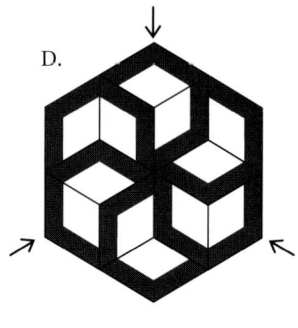
D.

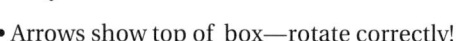

- Arrows show top of box—rotate correctly!
- Follow the arrows carefully while constructing 24B and 24C.
- Check the position all dark values as shown for 24D.

SPECIAL EFFECTS

COLOR WHEEL AND SPLIT CLUSTERS

1. Make one hexagonal cluster per color family for a total of six hexagonal clusters—one each for red, orange, yellow, green, blue and purple. Follow the diagram (Figure 24).
2. Use 12 additional diamond 9-patch units—two per color family—to create the center cluster (Figure 25).
3. **Split Clusters:** If creating split color clusters (**Quilt D**), follow the divisional guide for each color (Figure 26A & B).

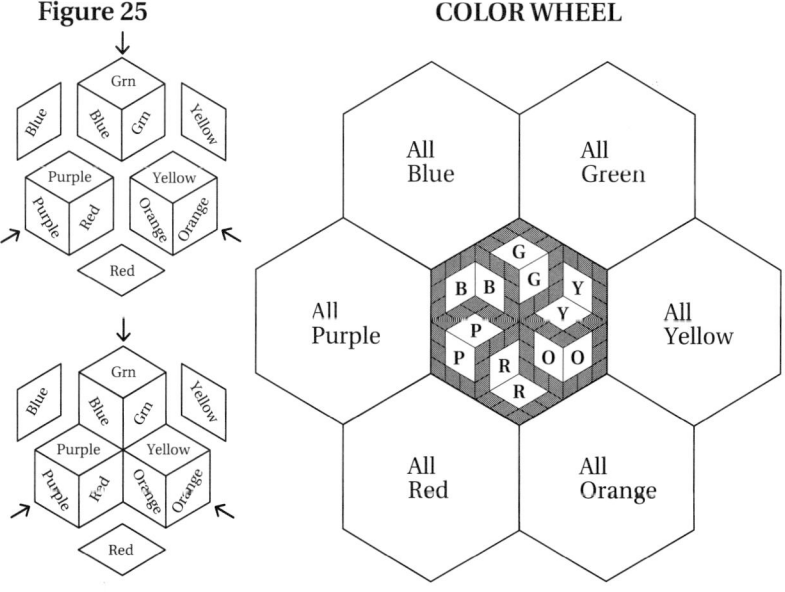

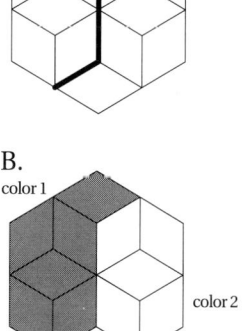

BACKGROUND SHAPES

ARRANGING THE HEXAGONAL CLUSTERS

Determining the final overall shape of your quilt requires arranging the hexagonal clusters into a relationship that pleases you. View the photographed **Quilts A, B, C** and **D** for different ideas, or create your own. Once your arrangement has been designed, sew the clusters together leaving the appropriate inset areas 1/4" unsewn.

Figure 27
Method 1

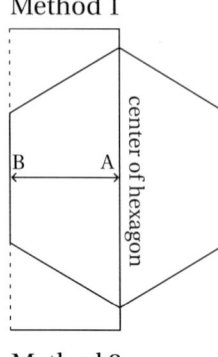

Method 2

Background fabric shapes must be cut and sewn (inset) around the perimeter of the quilt to finalize the quilt shape. An assortment of shapes may be necessary. They must be cut to fit the hexagonal clusters that you have created. The five background shapes are identified below. The *process* for determining their size, and the *techniques* used to cut them are called **Rotary Magic©**. Each is part is illustrated below..

DETERMINING THE CUT SIZE

In order to cut fabric shapes the correct size for everyone who creates this pattern, a technique of "measure and tailor" is identified. These "measure to determine" and "cut to fit" instructions are a unique bonus of all Doheny Publications books and patterns. They assure every quilter of continued accuracy and success for all sewing efforts regardless of the individual 1/4" sewing "error factor" we may have.

Iron the cluster well before taking any measurements. With the hexagon positioned "point" up, measure the hexagonal cluster you have sewn. Use a wide ruler as shown and measure from the center seam over to the raw outside edge *exactly*, using either ruler Method 1 or 2 (Figure 27). Make a note of this exact measurement.

For 1½" cut strips, the approximate measurement will be between 4½" to 6½".
For 2" cut strips, the approximate measurement will be between 17½" to 19½".
NOTE: **It does not matter what measurement you have, always use *your* measurement to figure and cut the necessary background fabric shapes.**

There are five basic background shapes:

1. Full Diamonds    4. Quarter Diamonds
2. Half Diamonds (*head to toe*) 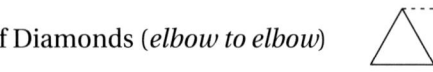   5. Oversized Corners
3. Half Diamonds (*elbow to elbow*)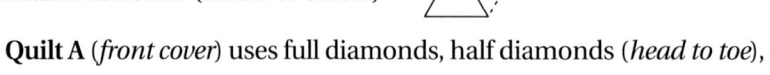

- **Quilt A** (*front cover*) uses full diamonds, half diamonds (*head to toe*), and half diamonds (*elbow to elbow*).
- **Quilt B** (*inside front cover*) uses full diamonds, half diamonds and oversized corners.
- **Quilt C** (*inside back cover*) uses full diamonds.
- **Quilt D** (*back cover*) uses full diamonds.

Figure 28

A. To determine strip **width** refer to specific background shape

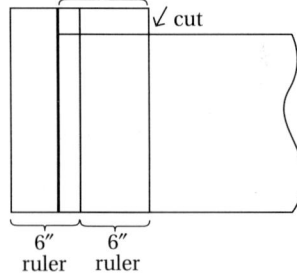

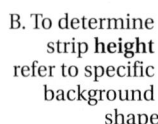

CUTTING THE BACKGROUND SHAPES

1. *With the exception of the full diamond,* the cut sizes have been *slightly* increased to allow for trimming later at all outside edges. The full diamond information will produce the exact sized diamond required. *You do not want this shape oversized.*

2. **Use two 6" rulers side by side to cut large strips and large diamonds** (Figure 28).

3. Always use *your* A to B measurement for each of the following procedures.

B. To determine strip **height** refer to specific background shape

C. Establish a 60° end angle

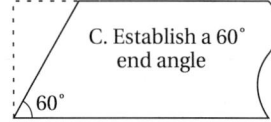

D. To determine **counter-cut width** refer to specific background shape

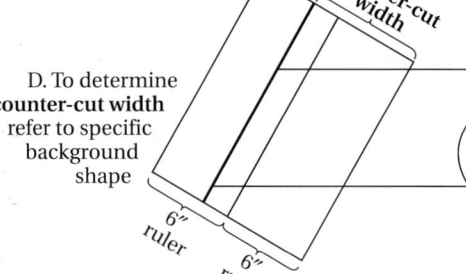

1. For Full Diamonds
    a) Take the A to B measurement and **add 1/4″**.
    b) Cut strips this size.
    c) Establish a 60° end angle
    d) Cut parallel using the same measurement, A to B + 1/4″
2. For Half Diamonds (*head to toe*)
    a) Take the A to B measurement and **add 1¼″**.
    b) Cut strips this size.
    c) Establish a 60° end angle
    d) Cut parallel using the same measurement, A to B + 1¼″.
    e) Counter-cut again on the head to toe diagonal of all diamonds. Each diamond yields two half diamonds.
3. For Half Diamonds (*elbow to elbow*)
    a) Take the A to B measurement and **add 1¼″**.
    b) Cut strips this size.
    c) Establish a 60° end angle
    d) Cut parallel using the same measurement, A to B + 1¼″
    e) Counter-cut again on the elbow to elbow diagonal of all diamonds. Each diamond yields two half diamonds.
4. For Quarter Diamonds
    a) Take the A to B measurement and **add 2¼″**.
    b) Cut strips this size.
    c) Establish a 60° end angle
    d) Cut parallel using the same measurement, A to B + 2¼″.
    e) Counter-cut again *on both diagonals*—head to toe, and elbow to elbow. Each diamond yields four quarter diamonds.
5. For Oversized Corners
    a) Take a "rough" measurement of the width and height of the missing area (Fig. 29).
    b) Add 2″ to each measurement.
    c) Cut two rectangles exactly the measurements H+2″ x W+2″ (Figure 30).
    d) Place the 60° angle of the ruler at the H-edge with the long edge (of the ruler) going *just below* the lower corner indicated by the dot "•" (Figure 31).
    e) Cut the rectangle as shown to create two triangles. The lower triangle is the correct size. Use it as a guide to trim the upper triangle correctly. These two triangles are now identical.
    f) Opposite triangles are also required. To create opposite triangles, cut the second rectangle with the opposite diagonal fracture (Figure 32).

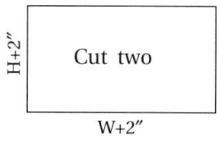

Fig. 29

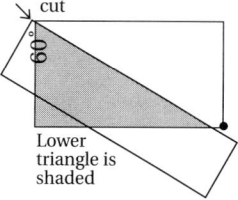

Fig. 30 Cut two

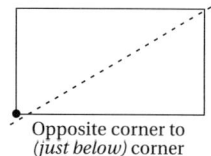

Fig. 31 Lower triangle is shaded

Fig. 32 Opposite corner to (*just below*) corner fracture

FINALIZING THE QUILTS

Add the background fabric shapes as necessary, following inset piecing guidelines. Several of the shapes are slightly over sized and will need to be trimmed at the external edge after they are inset. Be sure to *leave at least 1/4″ of fabric at the outside edge of the quilt to border and bind.* Finish your quilt as desired. Congratulations!

SPECIAL NOTE OF INTEREST

If you would like a special workshop on this or any other quilt pattern in the **Strata Art Quilt Series** for your guild or shop, feel free to contact Doheny Publications and request resumé information for Marilyn's national classes. All national classes feature wonderful slide presentations, "live quilts" and numerous options for every pattern in the series.

About the Author

Marilyn has always been both a people person and a fabric person. She started making quilts in 1982. The first of her three children was then nine months old, and she desperately needed an outlet with lots of adult interaction. So, to save her sanity and work with fabric, she enrolled in a six-week basic quilting course. During the entire six weeks, each student attempted to piece one pinwheel potholder using a single triangle template, then quilt it, and bind it. Truly, great things come from humble beginnings. Marilyn never finished that potholder (although it does hang, "in progress," on her sewing room wall). She was hooked and began to search the public libraries for books of quilt patterns. She then discovered that there are shapes other than triangles and was suddenly and overwhelmingly in love with the endless possibilities!

Since then, Marilyn's life has included every aspect of quiltmaking, from creating her own quilts to teaching others about the art. With joy and enthusiasm she has made hundreds of quilt tops and has inspired and instructed others to do the same. Marilyn is always dreaming up new patterns and inventing innovative sewing techniques for the traditional favorites. Her quilter's world is full of artistic achievements that "piece together" and give purpose to the joys of her life: color, texture, fabric, geometric patterns and people.

Other quality products from **Cutting Edge Quilt Designs**™ and **Doheny Publications**. Available at your local quilt store, or write to us at: P.O. Box 25151, Seattle, WA 98125

45° Kaleidoscope Wedge Ruler $16.96
Create clever, magical Kaleidoscope illusions fast and easily with this superb tool! Includes complete instructions with quick quilt pattern.

9° Circle Wedge Ruler $18.95
Infinite circular designs! Innovative new ruler includes instructions for 20 different patterns. Create spectacular quilts or clothing embellishments.

■ PATTERN BOOKLETS
featuring Marilyn Doheny's Rotary Magic© techniques for perfect cutting without templates

Amish Sparkle Star $6.95
A delightful interpretation of a traditional Amish pieced pattern.

Maple Leaves $6.95
Falling leaves is the motif of this wonderfully soothing quilt. Use up to 175 different fabrics for these 25 leaves — a great scrap quilt opportunity!

Trailing Vines $6.95
A glorious scrap quilt inspired by Susan McCord's antique quilt (1846), in the collection of the Henry Ford Museum. For hand or machine applique. Sections of the design can be used for clothing embellishments as well.

■ OTHER PATTERN BOOKLETS
Canadian Geese $7.95
Stunning, award-winning 52" quilt featuring two majestic Canadian Geese. Complete paper patch applique instructions.

Reticule $7.95
Original design of a "country lady's purse" used by women in the early 19th century to transport needle work projects. You will be delighted with its charming appearance as well as its remarkable usefulness. Quick and easy to sew. Includes instructions for three sizes.

Feathered Wishbone $4.95
Six versatile fine hand quilting motifs for blocks and borders

■ BOOKS
And if you enjoyed this book, other new titles from the **Strata Art Series—** *For Contemporary Eyes Only!* are:
Cubic Pinwheels $10.95
Cubic Ribbons $10.95
Triad Interlock $10.95
Woven Ribbons $10.95

Goosey Hearts $14.95
A lavishly illustrated 64-page book of original applique and hand quilting patterns featuring a full size fold-out of the Goosey Hearts quilt (38" x 28").

■ DESIGN ACCESSORIES
Kaleidoscope Design Grid $4.95
Graph paper featuring 4 and 6 division wedges for use with the 45° Kaleidoscope Ruler.

9° Circle Design Grid $4.95
The perfect accessory for designing elaborate spiral motion patterns for the 9° Circle Wedge Ruler.

Graph paper for the *Strata Art Series*
Triad Interlock Design Grid $4.95
Cubic Pinwheels Design Grid $4.95
Cubic Ribbons Design Grid $4.95
Woven Ribbons Design Grid $4.95

■ ROTARY CUTTING EQUIPMENT
Omnigrid™ **Ruler** 3" x 18" $8.95
6" x 24" $12.95
Olfa® Rotary Cutter (large) $15.95
Replacement blades (bulk 10) $36.00
Cutting Mat medium $21.50
large $39.00

Please send orders to:
Cutting Edge Quilt Designs™
P.O. Box 25151
Seattle, WA 98125

Include $1.50 shipping and handling for paper products;
$2.50 for rulers and cutting mats

Wholesale inquiries welcome.
Prices subject to change without notice.